In this WMG Writer's Guide, *USA Today* bestselling author Dean Wesley Smith takes you step-by-step through the stages most fiction writers go through and how not to lose hope along the way.

The
WMG Writer's Guide
Series

STAGES OF
A FICTION WRITER

KNOW WHERE YOU STAND
ON THE PATH TO WRITING

A WMG WRITER'S GUIDE

DEAN WESLEY SMITH

*wmg*PUBLISHING

Stages of a Fiction Writer

Published 2015 by WMG Publishing
www.wmgpublishing.com
Cover art © copyright Bswei/Dreamstime
Book and cover design copyright © 2015 WMG Publishing
Cover design by Allyson Longueira/WMG Publishing
ISBN-13: 978-1-56146-646-7
ISBN-10: 1-56146-646-8

First published in slightly different form on Dean Wesley Smith's blog
at www.deanwesleysmith.com in 2015

Writing into the Dark
copyright © 2015 by Dean Wesley Smith

Contents

STAGES OF
A FICTION WRITER

KNOW WHERE YOU STAND
ON THE PATH TO WRITING

A WMG WRITER'S GUIDE

INTRODUCTION

About twenty-five years ago, I was struggling to figure out where I was on the path to becoming a fiction writer.

I had sold novels, lots of short stories, been an editor, owned a publishing company, and had readers buying my books.

But honestly, none of that mattered to me. I liked it, sure, but my goal was to be a better writer, a better storyteller, actually. And I had no idea at all where I was at on the road to that goal.

Not clue one.

For the previous twenty years, as my skills grew, I had also been studying other writers and trying to understand how they did what they did.

I was typing in other writers' work to try to learn their tricks and their craft. I was reading every how-to-write book I could find.

But I still felt flat lost. I felt I had advanced, that I was past the basics, but what world did I have ahead of me with storytelling that I couldn't see?

I am the type that likes to look out ahead. But with storytelling, it was just a wall of mist.

So for my own use, I started to put this "Stages of a Fiction Writer" together.

I made the mistake, early on, of presenting some of this at a writer's workshop. Some of the members got very angry. And I do mean very.

I was kicked out because of my "attitude" and putting others down.

I had no intention of putting anyone down.

Seemed I had presented this wrong. But it was a work in progress.

And it wasn't until almost ten years later, about fifteen years ago now, that it all finally came together and made sense to me.

So a few years back, I did this as a lecture through WMG Publishing and put it up. It is still up as a lecture. But now I thought it might be time to get this into a book.

Knowing where I was at in learning storytelling, and where I could go if I kept practicing and learning, for me was very freeing.

Where Are You Going as a Writer?

Not a lot of writers give this much thought beyond the "I want to sell more and make a living."

Or… "I want a lot of people to read my books and be read in a hundred years."

Great hopes and dreams.

We all have those.

Nothing at all wrong with them.

But they sure don't help me in trying to figure out in general, where each of us stand as a storyteller.

Now, there are basics in all this that I am going to state and more than likely repeat numbers of times.

First... Continued learning of craft is critical.

I can't even begin to count the hundreds, maybe thousands of great writers who started to sell, thought they had it made, that they knew it all, and stopped learning. Now they are "Whatever Happened To" writers.

Learning can never stop. And if you have that attitude of learning is critical, then you can learn what it will take to move up stages.

Second... You can never learn it all when it comes to the craft of fiction writing.

This is sort of a shadow of the first point. The moment you think you have learned it all, that's where you freeze down. And that's where your career will remain until the craft of storytelling passing you by and no one buys your work anymore.

So where are you going as a writer?

That question assumes an end goal.

There is no end goal.

My answer is always, "Forward, to keep learning, and become a better storyteller."

My real end goal is to be challenging myself with a new story and a new way of telling it when I fall over dead.

A Poker Metaphor

In this book, I'm going to use poker playing as a metaphor to help be clear on some of the areas I am talking about. It is a very clear metaphor to how writers work.

Don't worry, I will make sure I explain poker clearly all the way. You do not need to be a professional poker player to understand this.

Or have even picked up a deck of cards. I promise to make it clear.

Why poker?

For most of my life, I played professional cards in one aspect or another. I started by playing gin rummy in the early 1970s, mostly in back rooms at golf clubs and in tournaments in Las Vegas.

I also played blackjack, and was a fan of Edward Thorp's 1966 book called *Beat the Dealer.*

Yes, I learned how to count cards.

When I went back to college in the early 1970s, I joined a blackjack team and paid my way through college completely playing on one team for a few years, then another for law school. I never told anyone I was doing that and had a couple part-time jobs to pretend I was earning money for college.

I also started playing poker in Las Vegas in the early 1970s and then off and on through the years after that, usually after the team was finished and headed home, I stayed a little longer to play some poker.

About twenty years ago, I picked up playing blackjack again at a local casino (not card counting, just playing tournaments) and then migrated to the poker room.

Then, at one point, disgusted with what was happening in traditional publishing, I basically quit writing and played professional poker to make a living. I did fine for a few years, playing mostly tournaments and writing a short story here and there along the way.

It was at a poker table about fifteen years ago in Las Vegas that I finally understood the **Stages of a Fiction Writer.**

And from that moment forward, I knew where I was going with my writing, what I was working toward.

Sure, book sales are great, but for me, I am happy with telling a good story. A story I feel as if I did my best with for the level of storyteller I am at the moment.

A Word of Warning

Because of the reaction to one of my first attempts at explaining this, I now understand that writers sometimes do not want to know where on the path they stand.

Mostly, of course, this is new writers who are in a hurry. Writers who get angry at this are writers who think that they should be able, with a few rewrites, to write a novel that will sell more than Stephen King and Nora Roberts combined.

And they are convinced they are better writers than those two as well as all bestsellers.

Uh, delusional, but that's the belief system.

Well, with a ton of luck, I suppose that could happen. But I always bet on skill and patience and learning.

At poker tables, when some really bad poker player was on a run of luck, and being obnoxious about it, I would say to the person, "Just hold on to those chips a little longer. They will be coming back my way shortly."

And they always did, because luck is both good and bad and evens out in the fairly short run. Skill and craft and learning will always win out over time. That's why poker is considered a sport, not a gambling game.

Skill wins.

So if you see yourself and your skill level at a certain point and it makes you angry, I am sorry. None of this is meant in any way to be personal.

This is meant to try to help the writers who want to move forward to understand what is ahead.

This is meant to pull back the mist a little and let writers peek into the minds of long-term professional writers.

And to help writers reach their dreams.

CHAPTER ONE

There are four basic stages of commercial fiction writing that are pretty clear. For this book, I just number them one through four.

I kind of think of them as places where writers live.

Basically, I'm an early-to-middle stage four writer. So is Kris. And we're working to get better all the time, as we always have.

Writers start in stage one and eventually work up into stage four if they keep learning and don't quit.

These stages will often have traits that carry over from one stage to another.

The lines between the stages are not dark and concrete, but are transitions that often take time to cross.

All of us, without exception, go through the early stages of fiction writing. No way around it.

And often writers can spend decades moving through a stage.

Or get stuck and have their career end in a stage.

So another way to think of this is like a journey.

A journey without an end point.

You never arrive, you never know it all as a fiction writer. Learning continues.

The key is never stop on the road. Keep moving and learning.

A Chess Example

To try to understand some of what I am talking about in coming chapters, keep in mind chess.

Those who have never played chess, or only played a few games, might know the moves of the pieces. But they can watch two chess masters and not have a clue what the masters are doing. The game is played on other levels than the prescribed moves of pieces.

When a beginning writer looks at a long-term bestseller, it is impossible to see what that writer did for book after book to get millions of readers every book. The books are just words, put into sentences. Right?

How hard can that be?

And chess pieces are just game pieces that move.

Just keep that in mind.

I Want to Jump Ahead Some Stages

Well, no. This question always comes up. No matter how much a beginning writer wants to get lucky and hit with some top selling books, which does happen, the skill level doesn't jump ahead.

We all go through the stages.

No matter how much of a hurry the writer might be in. And stage one writers are always in a hurry.

Now, that said, paying the price in the stages, the learning required to move through an early stage, can come from other places.

Often nonfiction professional writers can make a jump to professional fiction quicker. They might not be in the same stage with their fiction writing as they are with their nonfiction writing, but they can move quicker and start higher because they have "paid the price" in learning in nonfiction.

This also applies to those who started off writing plays, those writing for Hollywood, those coming out of advertising writing, and so on.

For those, the early stage or two were learned in other areas.

Stage One Fiction Writers

I went through this stage. We all start in stage one. I was no exception, never met an exception who didn't have a stage one period in one area of writing or another.

So what is a stage one commercial fiction writer? How can we spot stage one fiction writers?

Stage one writers believe fiction writing is sentences and grammar and punctuation.

That simple. The focus is sentence-by-sentence only.

Early on, all of us went through this. I was stuck in this period for seven years, from 1974 to January 1, 1982.

So what are some of the major traits that make you a stage one writer? Here are four major areas that might tell you if you have stage one issues or not.

1. Rewriting to Excess

The term many stage one writers use is "polish" when talking about this extreme rewriting.

Think rocks, folks, to understand this. You find a beautiful rock on the beach. It has color, it has sharp corners, it is unique. It drew your attention, after all, and made you pick it up.

So you are a stage one writer. You get home, toss that rock into a rock polisher, let it run with a bunch of other rocks, being polished down until finally, when it is finished, it is smooth and round and looks like all the poor other rocks you tossed in there with it.

With excess polishing of a story, you grind down any thought of originality, any possibility of author voice, and make the story same.

Sameness is dull.

A stage one writer's entire focus is on the words.

Stage one writers think that polishing the words makes for a better story. That is the belief.

It is wrong, but it is believed by millions.

Again, we all started there.

2. Extremely Slow

Even though stage one writers are in a hurry to be successful, by the very nature of stage one writing, of focusing only on the words and not story, stage one writers produce very little, if anything.

And that fits the myth that writing slowly means writing better stuff. (That shows no understanding of how the creative brain works. None.)

In the seven years I was stuck in this stage, I managed to produce two highly-polished short stories per year. And I was pretty focused at writing. Of course, all the stories were dull, no voice, no originality.

I had polished all that out in rewrites.

For seven years, I listened and tried to learn how to write from people who didn't know how to write creatively. I listened to every myth. There wasn't a myth I didn't buy into and try to do.

I was very, very slow. And I felt happy to get those two "perfect" stories out every year.

By all the myths, I was doing it right.

Sold nothing.

Had no career.

Of course, for stage one writers, it's always someone else's fault that they don't understand their perfectly polished story. Or it is some marketing thing now in indie that isn't working, and so on and so on.

Stage one writers always have an excuse for nothing selling.

Stage one writers believe they produce perfect stories and won't let anything but perfect out the door. So, of course it has to be someone or something else's fault their perfect story doesn't get the attention it deserves.

Of course.

And yup, I was no exception to that.

Seven long years.

3. Peer Writers' Workshops

Stage one writers tend to be in peer writer's workshops. And they often tend to write for the other members of the workshop.

They let someone who hates commas influence their work, or someone who hates too much setting up front change all their work.

This is like having ten different English teachers feed myths at you all at once.

Death of any good storytelling.

Total death.

And stage one writers tend to listen to suggestions from their workshops and then try to "fix" their story to make it better.

Yeah, writing by committee always produces great art.

Not.

There are "workshops" done by professionals, like the online workshops we do at WMG Publishing or Superstars done by Kevin J. Anderson or workshops done by Dave Farland, to name just three. If you find a workshop that is taught by someone who has been writing books for thirty years, those have value.

At our coast workshops, we don't let the other writers attending even speak about stories, even though most of them are selling professional writers. The only opinion that matters is the long-term professional instructors.

And we never let anyone teach who hasn't had a career in fiction writing in one area or another.

But peer workshops that are only full of stage one writers often will continue for a writer into early stage two before the writer finally goes, "that's silly."

I was attending workshops up into stage three, but only for quick audience reaction and learning business.

I never once tried to rewrite a story to the suggestion of a workshop. I at least managed to avoid that trap for myself. About the only one I missed along the way. I never found a peer workshop in my first seven years, thankfully.

And by the time I was into stage two and three, I mailed stories to editors before I ever took them to a workshop. That's why I learned that advice from workshops often kill stories. I sold a bunch of the stories that workshops told me sucked.

Luckily I mailed my story and didn't listen to people in workshops other than as a general audience reaction.

4. Concerned Only About Typing

Stage one writers have no idea at all about the look of a manuscript and how it relates to the story being told.

If they were taught in English class to put a paragraph every five lines, they do that. If they were taught that subject sentences are the key and can't do a paragraph until you get done with the subject sentence, they do that, having paragraphs that can often stretch for a page or more.

The idea of characters is not really formed for stage one writers, although stage one writers give voice to characters, but no learning about how to really do characters.

Stage one writers do character sketches ahead, thinking that's how it's done. And they mostly outline everything to death and follow their outlines because that's how it's done as well.

Pacing is an alien concept that might as well live on Mars.

Stage One Summary

Stage one writers have a focus only on the sentences, the grammar, the polish of a manuscript.

They give lip service to better characters, endings, and so on, but will spend ten drafts getting that "perfect" first line because they heard somewhere that was important.

All writers live for a time in stage one, or live in it while studying in other areas such as plays or nonfiction.

Some writers, with luck, go through it quickly.

Some of us, me included, take longer.

I really wanted to believe the myths that English teachers were teaching me. Desperately I wanted to believe them.

And I did, for seven long years.

But Dean, Didn't You Sell Two Short Stories in 1975?

Yes, I did. I was writing poetry at the time and selling it.

For my poems, I would struggle and rewrite a major "important" poem to death, work on a second one sort of, and then do a fun quick knock-off poem and then send all three poems out together.

I always sold the knock-off.

I never sold a poem I had worked on and rewritten. Thirty-some of the knock-off poems sold and I never caught a clue. My "good poems" didn't sell, and I stopped mailing poems in early 1976 to focus completely on fiction.

Well, somewhere in 1975 was when I first decided I wanted to try fiction.

So I wrote a quick story on my typewriter.

One draft.

Mailed it, no rewrite. (I had not yet bought into all the myths. I didn't know them, to be honest.)

Then I wrote a second story. Also fairly short.

One draft.

Mailed it.

Both of them sold right out. I had let the rough edges stay, my voice stay, my originality stay. Editors liked them and bought them.

Go figure.

Then, because they sold and I wanted to get better, I started learning the myths. And I started down into rewriting everything to death and writing slowly and focusing only on the words and sentences.

And seven years later I hadn't sold another thing.

For seven years I never put that together. Either with the poems I sold or with the two stories I sold. I was blinded by myths.

Completely.

And that's why I do the *Killing the Sacred Cows of Publishing* books. To help writers speed up through stage one.

CHAPTER TWO

Stage two of commercial fiction writers is again a stage we all go through. I was no exception, never met a writer who missed this one.

However, many writers can go through this stage quickly, often in a year or so. But at the same time, this is the place many, many millions of writers get stuck and eventually give up without ever reaching stage three and selling stories.

For lack of a better way of putting this, stage two is a transition stage.

The Major Traits of Stage Two Writers

—Focus is still solidly on the words.

—Writers are starting to see a change where the focus is shifting to understanding characters, plot, setting, and the other elements of a story. But again, the major focus is at the words and polishing to try to achieve characters, plot, setting and so on.

—Story is playing more of a part, but only slowly.

In other words, this is when writers start bringing their focus up and off the words and toward writing stories with real characters, emotional details, and so on. These are the early days of learning all this, but now the stage two writers are looking for answers, knowing that only focusing on the words no longer helps.

My *Twilight Zone Magazine* Stories

Now, as a stage three writer, later on, I ended up selling to the *TZ Magazine* and its sister magazine *Night Cry*. But something happened as a late stage one and early stage two writer to me with the magazine that bumped me solidly into stage two and then quickly beyond into stage three.

Back in 1981, the *Twilight Zone Magazine* started a new writer contest. At this point I had been a stage one writer for going on seven years, polishing and rewriting and thinking my work could easily win this new contest in this new magazine.

So I wrote them two stories for the contest. Almost an entire year's output in six months for me at that time and I was convinced both would win one award or another.

That fall I got the responses: Two form rejections.

(In hindsight, that's what the stories deserved because I had polished and polished anything original out of those two stories. They looked like everything else coming through the door to Ted Klein.)

But wow was I angry.

I blamed everyone else and decided to quit writing. What was the point if my brilliance would never be found? I had given it seven years, after all.

Then one fine night at a science fiction fan meeting that was being held in my bookstore, someone said something about how Ray Bradbury wrote stories.

And then another conversation came up about how Harlan Ellison had just sat in a bookstore window and wrote a story that had won a major award without rewriting it.

So something finally clicked in my thick skull and I started finally researching how other professional writers actually did it. **Not how English teachers had taught me it was done, but how real professionals worked.**

And then I found Heinlein's Rules.

Now I have a lecture through WMG Publishing about Heinlein's Business Rules, and at some point I might write a book about them. But at that point in the late fall of 1981, finding Heinlein's Business Rules sort of snapped my eyes open.

They were from a book in 1947 and they seemed so simple. But Heinlein in the article said the five simple rules were extremely difficult to follow, which is why there were so many aspirants who wanted to be writers and why there are so few professional writers.

I was, after seven years, damned tired of being an aspirant.

So as a New Year's resolution in 1982, I would follow Heinlein's Rules. I would write and mail a short story per week following the rules.

No exception.

One year later I was selling regularly and I have followed those simple rules ever since.

Five simple business rules.

And I agree with Heinlein. Almost no one can follow those rules. Everyone can make excuses that sound perfectly logical for them so they don't have to follow them.

But almost no one can follow those five simple rules.

Heinlein's Rules:
1. **You must write.**
2. **You must finish what you write.**
3. **You must not rewrite unless to editorial request.** *(Editors are people who buy things, not someone you hire, folks.)*
4. **You must put your work on the market.**
5. **You must keep it on the market.**

The moment I started following those rules, I moved quickly from stage one into stage two and then by 1983, about a year later, I had moved solidly into stage three and was selling.

Why? Because the rules forced me to stop focusing on the words and focus on writing stories.

If you are not focusing on words, what else can a writer focus on?

Answer: All the thousands of elements of storytelling, that's what.

The Monster Problem in Stage Two

Where millions and millions of writers get stuck and then quit in stage two is right at the focus point. They start to focus on the craft of storytelling, but they can't let go of the strong desire to only pay attention to the words.

After all, they ask, isn't writing typing words?

Stage two writers in this stage still write with grammar checker and spellchecker turned on.

Stage two writers are in a battle in their own minds. They are aware of the need for story and great characters and so on, and are learning them by taking workshops and buying how-to-write books.

But at the same time they cannot let loose of the intense myth that rewriting is critical, that every story must be polished.

So they learn character, then kill the story, learn great setting, then kill it by taking out character voice and so on, which is critical to setting.

To get out of stage two, you must slowly release the focus on words and realize they are just tools to use.

Carpenter Tools Analogy

Your desire is to be a fine cabinet craftsperson. So you focus on learning how to use hammers correctly. All the different types of hammers used to build finely crafted cabinets.

You become an expert with hammers.

But you think that learning hammers, learning how to pick the correct hammer for the job needed is **all that is required** to building a finely crafted cabinet.

You have been told over and over (by people who don't build cabinets) that to build a great cabinet, you must keep your hammers polished.

So you try to build a cabinet, but all you keep doing is when something goes wrong in construction, you go back and focus on your hammers and polish them some more. Must be the hammer's fault, after all.

Sound silly?

Well, everyone in stage two knows how to write a sentence, has grammar and spelling under control enough to check spelling when a manuscript is finished. That was all learned in stage one.

So now put the words, the sentences, in your tool box and move your focus completely to learning construction.

You must learn to trust your tools in stage two.

You must let go of the focus on the tool and just trust that in the process of writing, the tool will be there when you need it.

That's how you get out of stage two.

Ignore the typing, focus on the story, kill any idea of polishing.

And every time you have the need to go polish a story, just think of a cabinetmaker looking at his poorly constructed and designed cabinet and then polishing his hammers.

That won't fix the cabinet.

And polishing your words won't fix your story either.

Summary of Stage Two

Stage two is a transition stage.

It is when a writer takes the focus only on the words and polishing the words and moves that focus slowly to learning story and characters and setting and the thousand other basic details that go into being a great storyteller.

The writer is moving from someone who only pays attention to typing to paying attention to story.

Many writers take about a year to move from full focus on typing to full focus on story.

But many writers never learn to trust their tools. Many writers never learn that the tools are there and just need to be used when the creative voice wants to use them. And not thought about other times.

Millions and millions of writers quit right here in this stage.

I was almost one of them.

CHAPTER THREE

As we move into stage three, it's time I bring in the poker analogy I promised earlier on in the book.

As I said, I have always had cards in my life. I paid most of my way through college with cards, and also played professional poker for a time.

The definition of a professional poker player is a person who makes most of his or her money playing poker. I am now a semi-professional since I make money at poker when I play, but I make most of my money these days from my writing.

In fact, here in 2015 I don't play much poker at all. Occasional trips to Las Vegas is all. I might go back more in the coming years. Time will tell.

But this poker analogy works very, very well. The stages of poker are almost exactly parallel to the stages of writing, and you don't need to know poker to understand the analogy. Honest.

For this analogy, I'm going to use the poker game called Texas Holdem. (Yes, spelling can be Hold 'em or Hold'em, but for this, I'll use the simple spelling.)

Texas Holdem is a seven-card game to make the best five-card poker hand.

At the start, each player around a table (usually 9 at a full table) is dealt two cards down, so only the player can see them.

There is a betting round.

The dealer places three cards face up in the middle of the table. (All players use those three cards.)

Another betting round.

The dealer places one more card face up on the table.

Another betting round.

The dealer places the last card face up on the table.

Last betting round.

All players are trying to make the best five-card poker hand from the five public cards and the two private cards in their hands.

Stage One Poker Players

Stage one or beginning poker players often don't even know a good poker hand or what beats what. They have no idea if the two cards that only they can see are good or not, and have no awareness of anyone else around them in any real fashion.

They might have seen a major player win with a certain hand on television and think that's a good hand without knowing why or how to even play it.

The focus of a stage one poker player is only on their two cards in their hand.

If they think those two cards are good, nothing else matters. Nothing.

Just as stage one writers only have a focus on the words on the page with no real awareness beyond the words.

If a stage one writer thinks the words are perfect, the grammar correct, all commas are in the right place, then the story must be perfect.

Of course, just as stage one writers find no readers, stage one poker players often have no idea why a pot with their money in it is awarded to another player. After all, they had an ace in their hand. Isn't an ace good?

Yup, about as good as having all the commas correct in a story.

Stage Two Poker Players

When a poker player moves into stage two, they are still, just as writers, focused far, far too much on the two cards in their hand that the other players can't see.

But awareness for the stage two player is starting to expand.

Stage two players can actually see the cards on the table and put them with their cards and maybe realize that their cards can't win in some situations.

Stage two poker players still lose far more than they win, but their awareness and knowledge is expanding. It is a transition stage, just as with writing.

Think of a bubble of awareness.

In stage one, the bubble was over the player only and his two cards. In stage two, the bubble of awareness has expanded out to include the cards face up on the table and knowing poker hands and so on.

In stage two writing, the focus is still solidly on the words. But the awareness has expanded out to include character and story to some degree. But when in doubt, the stage two writer always falls back on the words, trying to rewrite to fix a story.

You see this a lot in stage two poker players in things like the following example:

A player has two cards in his hand that combined with three other cards face up on the table make a straight. A straight is a decent hand, right?

Sure, but not when there are four cards on the board that are hearts. (A flush beats a straight.)

And even though the player has no hearts in his hand, he will call bets thinking he might win. That's like a stage two writer having a story fail and thinking if he just rewrites it, all will be fine.

The straight won't win against a flush and rewriting won't help a story.

The bubble of focus is still far too tight.

Stage Three Poker Players

I'm going to give the poker analogy before I start talking about stage three writers.

Think of the bubble of awareness I mentioned above. In stage three poker players, the awareness bubble has expanded to include everyone at the table.

Inside the awareness bubble, the player is watching what other people bet, how they play, what kind of hands they play regularly.

Often stage three poker players know or think they know what another player's two hidden cards are, and act on that knowledge.

The stage three poker player still has a focus on his own two cards, but has no problem in throwing away his two cards at the hint of a loss, and just not even playing for many hands in a row if good starting hands do not appear.

Stage three poker players understand the game, can glance at the five cards on the table and tell you what the best possible hand is for those five cards.

24

Stage three poker players can win, sometimes more than they lose overall depending on what level of stage three they are in, and who they are playing against.

Many, many professional poker players never leave stage three playing level. They don't need to. They are making a living.

So the awareness bubble has expanded out to everything on the table and the other people playing.

Still some focus on the cards, but the cards are more of a tool that a stage three player can take or leave, depending on the game, the stakes, and the others playing.

Cards in the hand are still important, but not critical anymore.

However, a stage three player would never think of playing a hand of cards without looking at the two cards they have. (Keep that in mind in a future chapter.)

Stage Three Writers

Think of the awareness bubble.

In stage three writers, the awareness has expanded out.

Now the awareness is on telling a good story, on having an interesting plot, on doing great openings, on writing great characters, on getting a reader into a story and holding them in the story.

Words now are still important, but only in the service of the story and nothing more.

Words can be tossed away at will, just as cards are tossed away in poker.

Traits of solid stage three writers:

—They have command of many, many different tools of writing that come out of the words and use those tools when needed. They no longer focus on the words. They only use the words.

—They have a solid grasp of story, of character, and of setting. And are constantly trying to get better at all three.

—They understand copyright and the business and sales. In other words, awareness is off the words and out into the world.

—They are writing at a decent pace.

—They seldom rewrite if at all (in the traditional sense of the term rewriting). Early stage three writers will still rewrite at times to fix story, but middle and late third stage writers seldom rewrite.

—Late third stage writers have often been around for some time.

Third stage writers often can make a living with their work. There are lots of ups and downs, but if the writer can weather those early ups and downs in this stage and learn the business and keep learning how to be a better storyteller, they tend to last for a while.

Third Stage is a Burial Ground for Writers

Sad to say that most writers who hit early third stage tend to stop learning. And that's where they stop and freeze down.

Eventually, sales dry up, their publisher drops them, they can't sell more books or their indie sales are not good, and they give up and go away.

Often stage three writers feel like they know it all, make a few sales, and just move on to other things because writing is too hard.

Or they accomplished their dream. No point in going on.

The history of publishing is littered with three-and-four-book authors who vanished. More thousands than I would ever want to try to count, sadly.

And indie publishing is not going to help this in any fashion. Early stage three indie writers are going to make a little money, have a market change kill their sales, and the writers will leave, not understanding that learning and sticking with it can get them up to a more sustained sales and craft level.

The awareness bubble keeps expanding all the way through the different levels of stage three.

For me, it took from 1984 when I crept into the lower levels of stage three and started selling until about 2005 to move through the levels of stage three writing and finally break through into the next level.

And during all those years I kept learning, experimenting, studying other writers.

Stage three writing is the place where writers sell. And if you keep learning storytelling, adding tools to your craft, and learn copyright and the business, you can have a nice, solid career for a few decades in stage three.

But to really stick around and become an old professional and a bestseller, stage four needs to be your goal.

CHAPTER FOUR

Almost all writers reading this will be in stage three.

If you see yourself in stage one, all focused on the writing and polishing of words, you can move quickly out of that once you understand the location you are stuck in. And then start making changes.

Change your focus to story. Stop polishing. Let your voice come through.

And stage two is the transition stage from the focus on polishing to the focus on story and characters and so on.

Stage three is huge. It would be like crossing the United States and Australia combined. It's a ton of territory and a lot of things to learn. At one point someone suggested I try to break stage three down into levels and I just sort of laughed and shuddered at the same time.

Stage three is the learning and focus on story. On becoming a better storyteller.

I do entire workshops to try to help people move forward in just small areas of stage three such as character voice or depth or pacing or cliffhangers or ideas.

No way to break down stage three because one stage three writer will have a certain few skills mastered and be poor at others, while the writer sitting next to them will be poor at the skills the other writer has mastered.

Both writers are in stage three.

Expanded Awareness

As I detailed out in the poker analogy of stage three poker players being aware of everyone at the table and how they play, stage three writers are now gaining more and more awareness of story and business at the same time.

The bubble of awareness is just slowly expanding to include more and more skills that it takes to be a great storyteller and make money in this business of telling stories.

And the skills of sentence-by-sentence writing are more and more just taken for granted.

Sure, things like learning depth is a sentence-by-sentence skill in many ways, but it goes to the focus of story and character and reader reaction.

Understanding what a fake detail is might be down in the words, but it goes to story and character as well as reader reaction. What is learned in the basics of sentence writing in stage three all goes to service of story.

But the awareness bubble (for most writers) has limits.

And that is the problem.

The best way I like to describe this problem is that a writer walks into a huge lobby area of a building. As you first enter the building (or stage three) you have no idea at all that there are fifty or more stories of the building above that large lobby and the shops and stuff around the lobby.

The awareness bubble does not move past that one level. Writers just can't see the upper floors, and often don't even know they are there, let alone how to find a staircase or an elevator. They don't even realize they should look for one.

Writers at this level often stay in the lobby, happy with a few sales here and there.

Or they slowly become aware there is more above them, more things to learn. And these writers start looking for that staircase upward.

There are lots of floors of stage three above them. But sadly, most writers I have seen make the lobby and that's where they stay, eventually just drifting off into history.

My entire point of this book is in hopes that someone reading it is stuck in the lobby and realizes that they need to look for a staircase upward, that they need to get back to learning and studying other writers.

How do you find a staircase or elevator out of that lobby? By learning and studying and becoming aware that there are better writers out there than you.

And then studying them.

To find a way out of this huge lobby, you need to stop thinking that all long-term successful writers just got lucky and can't really write. Start asking yourself what is Cussler or Steele or Patterson or King or Oates doing right?

Get your taste out of the equation and study.

The staircase doors will start appearing.

And what is even more amazing, once you start climbing upward, you see things that you didn't even know existed. And the more that happens, the more you realize you really didn't know jack about telling stories.

How to Tell if You are In Stage Three?

Pretty simply, actually.

—Are you focused on learning story, learning character, learning depth, and on and on and on?

—Are you starting to have some success selling? Either indie or traditional.

—Do you have more than one or two books out?

—Have you cut down the number of rewrites, or found a better way, and want to get to the next story before you are almost done with the last one?

Death Spirals in the Lobby of Stage Three

There are three really, really common problems that early stage three writers have. In fact, I would say these two problems are the death of 95% of all stage three writers' careers.

It's like the writer gets into the lobby, looks around, and then turns and leaves.

Problem #1: Thinking that only original plots sell.

If you think this, wow do you need to really learn story and the history of story and so much more.

But the best way to do that is just stop thinking this and worrying about this. If you think all ideas are hard to come by and all need to be original, just take the Ideas online workshop that I do at WMG Publishing and I'll save you from this death in six short weeks. I promise.

I can hear the voices in your head saying, "But... but... but... I must have great ideas..."

That's your critical voice trying to slow you down, stop you, and if you let it, you are doomed from this one problem alone.

Problem #2: I don't need to learn that.

This is a thought pattern that gets nasty very quickly. It starts bringing in time and money and day jobs and so on and so on. This also is your critical voice trying to stop you or slow you down.

Critical voice only has one job and that's to stop you. Thinking you **DO NOT** need to learn something, anything, or practice something, is a golden road for your critical voice to stop you.

Learning never stops in this business.

Ever.

My suggestion is this: If you hear yourself say, "I'm good enough in that area to not worry about it now." Then notice you said that, stop, and focus on that area. Learn it, make sure your critical voice knows that every time it attempts to pull that trick on you, you will go learn what it is trying to keep you from learning to improve your skills and selling.

"Good enough" is deadly in writing.

Deadly.

Problem #3: Patience and lack of long-term perspective.

The thinking goes like this: *I've been at this long enough. It's not working. I've spent three years or five years or whatever at it. I need to walk away.*

Or even more stupid, sometimes I hear this expressed this way in the indie world: *My friends are all selling better than I am. I only made 300 sales last month, I'm failing, I'm going to quit.*

The door to the building is that big wide thing with people streaming in and out.

All long-term professional writers have learned to not be insulted by some two-or-three-year writer who proclaims they should be selling better than anyone. Or one of the one-or-two-year writers who got lucky with the right book at the right place and started selling quickly and think they are god's gift to writing.

I have worked since 1974 at this writing thing, learning and working and writing millions and millions and millions of words. When some three-year writer tells me I don't know how to write, or proclaims they are a better writer than Patterson, I just smile and turn away because I know they are already half-way out the door.

Harsh? Yes.

Not fair? Yes.

This is a business.

This is an art that takes decades to learn just the basics and you never learn it all. If you think you don't need those decades of learning because your English teachers told you that you had talent, then all I can say is "Goodbye."

I know that all beginning writers are in a hurry. I know that. I was as well.

So I suppose a true indication that you are well into stage three is that you understand the time needed to learn your art and business.

I hope you are not in any of those problems at the moment, or if you are, you can snap out of it, get back to learning, and expand your awareness to the fact that there are levels of writing you just can't see yet.

And then have the desire to see those new levels. After all, you made it through the first two stages. You can go higher and farther.

The Secret to Working Through Stage Three

Just tell the next story.

Do your best on every story you write, keep learning, keep practicing, and then just tell the next story.

Get that story you just finished out to sell to readers in one way or another.

And then just keep learning and tell the next story.
Make writing fun.
Make learning fun.
Make telling stories fun.

CHAPTER FIVE

Starting into stage four, the top stage.

I got a question after the last chapter when I put that chapter on my blog. "How many writers are in stage four?"

Think of stage four as a decent-sized town.

Selling stage three writers could fill a couple large cities. As I said earlier, most stage three writers never get past those first sales. To reach stage four, it takes an intense desire to keep learning and studying the art of storytelling.

And it flat takes years and years and millions and millions of words.

Sorry, just can't jump there. Not even slightly possible.

So What Is a Stage Four Writer?

—A writer in complete control of the art of storytelling.
—A writer who is still learning.

—A writer who is using techniques, often without knowing, that are advanced.

—A writer who is balanced in skills.

—A writer who has no giant weak areas in their storytelling.

—A writer who can handle any kind of storytelling technique a story demands.

—A writer who is a bestseller and has been for many, many years, if not decades.

—A writer who knows when a reader needs something before a reader knows they need it.

So what is the difference between stage three and stage four writers?

Often not much for advanced stage three writers. But still there are critical differences.

Stage three writers are often bestsellers, but fairly new at it. Stage three writers often have huge areas of their writing they are weak at and fear some types of storytelling.

Often a stage three writer will be very good at one area and will be using that all the time to keep selling without adding in the balancing skills.

And most importantly, a stage three writer is not always in control of a story. Not from a critical place, but from a skill place.

More importantly, stage three writers have very, very little awareness of readers on the other side of the story. They may think of readers in marketing, but never in telling their own stories.

How to Explain This

To make this clear, I need to go back to the poker analogy. (And please, any professional poker player out there, give me some slack. I am being general here in a hope to help writers, not other poker players.)

So I was there on the same table with two of the top players in the world for at least eight hours if I could survive. They did not know me. I was like the other players to them, but they clearly knew each other.

So I just sat back, made a clear point of looking at my cards each time, and then tossed them away. I didn't even care what they were.

I had no intention of playing for at least the first hour of the tournament. Not because I was afraid, but because I wanted to set something up for the two top players and watch how they played as well.

Seidel basically only played a few hands in the first hour and everyone folded to him.

On my right, Pham was raising almost every hand and pulling most of the small pots, only getting into a few fights at all with anyone at the table. And when Seidel was in a hand, Pham laid down his cards.

So finally, after one hour, Seidel and Pham clearly thought they had a clear read on me. They clearly thought EXACTLY what I wanted them to think.

I hadn't said a word, just folded every hand. They figured I was a tight player who was playing scared. I would have thought the same thing in their positions.

So after the first hour, on one hand, I glanced down and had a pair of kings. Pham raised, I re-raised him and everyone else on the table folded around to him. He nodded and without looking at his cards folded.

That one hand repaid all the blinds I had lost in the first hour.

What Pham was thinking was that I was a very tight player, an early stage player with a lot of patience, and would only play top hands, and Pham didn't want to fight with a top hand, especially so early in the tournament. (That was why I went with a pair of kings to start making my move, to make sure that if I did get called down to a showdown, I would have the powerful hand I wanted him to think I only played.)

I had made him believe he knew what cards I was going to play. And I noticed that when Pham folded, Seidel nodded. Seidel clearly had the same thought.

Two hands later, Pham raised again and I re-raised him again. This time I had two low garbage cards. But I knew he was a stage four player and all I cared about was what he thought I had, not what I actually had.

He folded again.

So for the next two hours, Pham took money from other players and I took money from him at times when he raised.

Not once did I get in a showdown with anyone in those first hours. Not one person ever saw my cards.

At that point in my life, I also had great peripheral vision and I raised Pham a couple of times when I noticed he hadn't even looked at his cards. I hadn't looked at mine, either, but that's beside the point. I was just playing with his mind.

In essence, we were playing cards without caring what our own cards were. Impossible to even imagine to a stage one or two poker player.

Players kept getting knocked out and leaving our table and leaving their chips behind with the three of us. At the lunch break, Seidel and Pham and I had the three large stacks.

After lunch, Pham changed his play from raising almost every hand and went to playing more like Seidel and I knew they had changed their read on me, so I changed to regular play, and the three of us took turns taking money from the others.

And never after lunch did I raise Pham or Seidel and they never raised me either. In other words, their read on me had gotten a little closer to my actual skill level and in the early hours of the tournament there was no reason to mix it up.

They knew exactly what I had done to them. I had led them to believe I was one type of player when I was actually another.

Mind control.

After nine hours, the tournament broke our table to send us to empty chairs at the twenty remaining tables. We walked together upstairs talking. (This was in Binions and I went back to writing shortly after that tournament and have never had the pleasure to sit at a poker table with either of them again.)

So the key to stage four poker players, when playing other stage four players or good stage three players, is to make the other player think they understand and know what you have.

How Does This Apply to Stage Four Writers?

Simple and exactly the same.

Stage one writers only worry about the typing. The words.

Stage two writers are starting to worry about story, but still focus on typing and the words.

Stage three writers have expanded out to be aware of story and characters and they notice pacing and so much more. (Remember, stage three is a huge area that takes years to get through and most never do.)

Stage four writers could not much care about the words. Words are in the complete control of stage four writers and are only part of the tools the writer uses.

What is important to a stage four writer is what the reader is experiencing at any given moment in the story.

In other words, stage four writers' awareness has expanded outside the words, outside the story, outside of characterization, and to what the reader will be thinking and feeling at any moment in the story.

Stage four writers understand what will hold a reader in a story, understand when a question needs to be answered and answer it a fraction of a second before the reader thinks it.

Stage four writers will not allow the reader out of the story, and so much more.

Just as I controlled Pham and Seidel's thoughts on that table for a few hours, stage four writers control readers' minds from word one of a story to the final word.

And often beyond.

CHAPTER SIX

Stage four in writing is hard, at best, to describe because for most writers, it is a level of craft that is impossible to see.

So how do you move through stage three and get to stage four writing?

Mostly, the answer boils down to one simple thing: Read.

Read for pleasure.

Then when you find a book that you really, really enjoyed, go back and study it until you understand what the writer did to hold you in the book, what made you enjoy the book besides the subject.

Study at different times all aspects of the book.

For example:

—Understand the many, many, many different types of cliff-hangers the author used.

—Understand the pacing of the scenes, the characters, the setting. (Yes, setting has pacing.)

—Understand the character voice, the cadence, the syntax, the pacing and choices of words and character tags.

—Understand the structure of the book, the movement through the book, the reason the author made the choices the author made.

You do all this after you read a book and really, really love it.

Read for pleasure, then study.

Who to Study?

This is where I am constantly shaking my head at newer writers. They are studying other newer writers.

Huh?

Newer writers are often stage three writers who had parts come together enough to make books work. If you are trying to stay in stage three, then study stage three writers.

If you are trying to move to stage four writing, study stage four writers.

Stage four writers are writers who have been producing for twenty or more years and who are bestsellers and write more than one book every few years.

Grisham is a great writer to study. You can see what he has done in his books and he is easy to study.

Koontz is a hard study because he's so subtle. But he, more than any other writer working today besides King, is a master of more techniques than you or I can ever imagine. So study him. His Odd Thomas books are great ones to study.

The list of stage four writers to study goes on and on.

Some bestsellers are not to your taste. Granted.

But if you think that a long-term bestseller such as Cussler can't write, and you are stage two or early stage three writer, you need to catch a very large clue.

And if you think Patterson can't write (when he writes alone), you need your writing mind examined.

Granted, long-term, major-selling stage four writers might not be to your taste. But they know what they are doing and you could learn from them if you open your mind.

There is a reason that hundreds of thousands of people buy every book a major bestseller puts out year after year for decade after decade. Figure out what that reason (actually it is a thousand writing skill reasons) is if you really want to get to stage four.

Study them.

And there are many stage four writers who fly under the radar for most people.

Many, many, many of us, actually.

A prime example is Joyce Carol Oates.

Another prime example is my wife, Kristine Kathryn Rusch.

Both would be worth your time to study. Those two write what they want and often the subject matter they tackle is not a subject that has a lot of readers. They don't care.

They write what they love and both have been major bestsellers for decades and both have won more awards than I can imagine. (And I see those awards stacked all over my wife's office and leaning against shelves and waiting to be framed and so on.)

In mystery, there are numbers and numbers of writers who are stage four and most students would not think to study them.

Lawrence Block, Edward Gorman, Barry Malzberg, to name just three of many.

Or study John D. McDonald's Travis McGee series. You'll have to reread those many times to start seeing the real genius of McDonald in those books.

Same guidelines on who to study applies to romance and westerns and so on.

So read for pleasure, study to advance your own art after enjoying a book.

Never study during a first read, unless a book is not to your taste subject-wise. For example, Danielle Steel is not to my taste, but I have purposely studied numbers of her books to really understand what she does and to learn.

Some Problem Areas Common in Stage Three Writers to Cure

Stage four writers are in control of their readers. Any reader in any walk of life or age or country.

Stage four writers control readers. Period.

Stage three writers are often writers who haven't learned even the basics of doing that.

A few examples:

—Fake Details.

Stage three writers often use fake details and thus lose control over their readers. Fake details come from stage one and stage two when writers think they need to add in setting, so they type it in instead of running the setting through the opinions and emotions of a character.

Example I use all the time in classes is the word "barn." A total fake detail because without emotions and descriptions through a character, every reader imagines a barn from his or her own past. And trust me, not all barns look the same.

The word "tree" is another commonly used fake detail. Example… *He walked among the trees.*

Check in with the image that appeared in your mind when I wrote that. It will be different for every reader.

But what I meant was… *He walked among the short Noble fir trees, brushing his hands over their tops gently, enjoying the silk feel of their needles and the thick smell of rich fir, knowing that in six months most of these tree would be gone, decorated with bulbs and lights in homes around the country and he would have enough money to barely live for yet another year.*

Yeah, trees is a fake detail unless you run it through the senses and emotions of a character.

Learning how to do that is just one step toward stage four.

One of many.

Another Major Area of Stage Four Writing

Pacing…

Pacing is an area of writing that is impossible to see until you reach a level of skill that allows the mind to understand just the lower levels of the skill and art of pacing.

Lower levels of pacing are often used, without knowing, by stage three writers.

Hitting the return key, understanding that content drives the look of the manuscript, the length of the sentences, the size of the paragraphs. Many stage three writers work into this knowledge in the later areas of stage three.

But there is so much more to pacing than just knowing where to put a period and when to hit a return key. Those basics must be learned first, granted. But let me give you an example of a higher level, stage four level, of pacing.

This one area is easy to see, but impossible to implement at first.

How to see this one area of pacing: Go to an airport, park yourself off to one side in a chair looking at a busy hallway. The best place is just outside a security area as people are moving from the ticket counter to security.

Now with only pacing in mind, watch the people. And watch the pacing of the writing.

***

A woman chicken-steps past in high heels.
Click. Click. Click. Click.
Very fast.
Pulling a carryon.
Intent. Gaze forward.
Often phone or ticket in hand.

***

Next a man in jeans, a jacket, and tennis shoes strides past, seemingly without a care in the world.

His gait looks long, his shoes make no sounds, his eyes up and looking ahead.

He wears a backpack and seems to be in no hurry at all, a smile on his face as he enjoys the walk like a day in the park.

***

Behind the strider comes a man in a fairly cheap, off-the-rack business suit.

Too much cologne drifts behind him like a toxic cloud.

He walks with purpose, his stride medium. His cheap (but polished) shoes make a thumping sound in the hallway.

His tie pulled up tight against his neck. His coat buttoned to prescription.

His phone against the side of his head.

His dark eyes intense.

He acts like the phone call signals the end of the world.

***

Characters have pacing, just as scenes, chapters, setting, and dialog have pacing.

Yeah, I know, seems impossible to just do, and it is impossible to do from the critical voice. And rewriting always kills such things.

This must all be learned and then come out of the creative voice.

And I'm not even going to try to explain things like story voice, story tone, genre tone, and so on into meta-details.

You'll get there if you read for pleasure and then go study.

The Key and a Focus Point to Move Forward

Stage four is about control.

Just as I used the stage four poker players as an example of how they try to control what others think they have, stage four writers are complete mind-control artists.

Stage four writers make sure that no matter what question in a story a reader has, it is answered at the right moment.

So to start working through stage three and toward stage four, start focusing on control.

Learn the basics of pacing, learn depth and how to control readers with your openings, learn how to relay details through emotions and setting.

Control.

Do three things:

—One, read for pleasure, then study books you have read for the learning.

—Open your eyes when out in the real world and start seeing other people and paying attention to them. Pay attention to the patterns and the tags and everything.

—Learn business as you go because all stage four writers know the publishing business. You might get to stage four writing levels, but it will do you no good in this new world if you are also not a stage four business person.

And no, there is no business in this book. This is a craft book. I just wanted to make sure to mention that right here because it is that critical.

Stage four writers are balanced in all their writing skill sets and in their business.

And they are in control of all of it.

Takes time and a lot of practice, but you can get there.

SUMMARY

As I have said a number of times, no writer skips over any of these four stages of a fiction writer. We all go through them starting at the beginning if we ever get to stage four, the top level of fiction writers.

However, along the way, sadly, millions of writers get stopped in chasing their dream of writing sellable fiction at one stage or another.

So this book was my attempt to detail out the road that fiction writers walk.

And maybe for a few writers give some hints as to what is ahead.

And for another few writers, help the realization of what is happening with their writing is normal.

The Four Stages Once Again

Stage one writers only worry about the typing. The words.

Stage two writers are starting to worry about story and character, but still focus on typing and the words.

Stage two writers are still lost in thinking that polishing a story will help it. But they are in transition from the first stage to the third stage.

Stage three writers have expanded out to be aware of story and characters and they notice pacing and so much more. (Remember, stage three is a huge area that takes years to get through and most never do.)

Stage three writers early on start to understand words are tools and by the end of stage three the writers are so focused on story they often no longer see the words. And seldom rewrite.

Stage three writers can make a living for a short time, but this stage is where most writers leave for a thousand personal reasons.

Stage four writers could not much care about the words. Words are in the complete control of stage four writers and are only part of the tools the writer uses. What is important to a stage four writer is what the reader is experiencing at any given moment in the story.

So think of the journey in this fashion...

A writer starts by focusing only on the tools, then expands out to learn aspects of telling stories and finally moves to a position of controlling readers' minds.

> **Stage one and two writers are typists.**
> **Stage three writers tell stories.**
> **Stage four writers are entertainers.**

It really is that simple.

And that hard.

I hope this book helps you with your journey. And can keep you moving forward and learning and having fun.

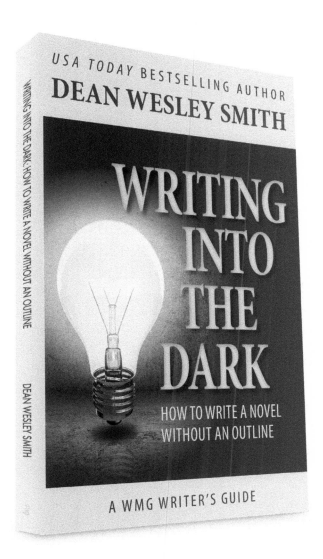

If you enjoyed *Stages of a Fiction Writer*,
you might also enjoy *Writing into the Dark*, available
now from your favorite bookseller.

Turn the page for a sample.

CHAPTER ONE

SOME BACKGROUND

The reason there are very few articles or books about writing into the dark is because the process gets such horrid bad press. Just the idea of writing without planning ahead on a project as long as a novel makes most English professors shudder and shake their head and turn away in disgust.

And beginning writers mostly just can't imagine doing that. It just seems impossible.

Yet, many long-term professional writers write this way. And many of the books those same English professors study were written completely into the dark.

So why do all of us, as we are growing up, buy into the idea that novels must be outlined to the last little detail to work?

First, the problem comes from the fact that we all started out as readers.

To readers, writers know it all. They know enough to make that plot twist work, that foreshadowing inserted at just the right place, the gun planted when it needs to be planted to be fired later, and so on.

To readers, writers are really smart to be able to do all that.

Then we get into school and all the English teachers build on that belief system by taking apart books and talking about the deep meaning and what the writer was doing. And that makes writers seem even smarter and the process of writing a novel even more daunting.

So the desire to outline is logical, totally logical, after all that.

In fact, it seems like outlining is the only way to do a complex novel.

But interestingly enough, that very process of outlining often kills the very complex structure the writer is hoping to achieve.

A HUMBLING EXPERIENCE

Two of the most humbling experiences in my life occurred the two times I went into a graduate-level English class at a university as a professional writer. (Do not do this if you can avoid it.)

The first time, the English professor, doing his job, had the students read and discuss two of my short stories BEFORE I GOT THERE.

So two of my stories were deconstructed by fifteen graduate English department students.

So I arrived, talked some about what it was like to be a freelance fiction writer, and then the professor turned the discussion to my two stories they had read. And I started to get questions about how did I know to put in the second hidden meaning of the story, or the foreshadowing of an upcoming event, or...or...or...

They all knew far, far more about those two stories than I did.

Honestly, I could barely remember the stories, and I had no idea I had even put in all that extra stuff they were all so impressed by.

And the reason I couldn't remember is that my subconscious, my creative brain, put all that in. My critical, conscious brain had nothing at all to do with it.

I had just let my creative brain tell a story.

Nothing more.

The problem was that for weeks after that first time into that class, I couldn't get all that crap back out of my head. I found myself wondering about second meanings, about subplots, about foreshadowing—all those other English-class terms. Froze me down completely until I got past it.

Let me be clear here. My critical brain is not smart enough to put all that stuff in. Luckily for me, my creative brain seems to be smart enough if I get my critical brain out of the way and let it.

But getting that stupid critical brain out of the way is the key problem.

BREAKING OUT OF THE TAUGHT PROBLEM

All of us go into writing novels with all that training of thinking we need to know all that stuff about subplots, foreshadowing, sub-meanings, and so on. Thinking about it, I find it amazing that with the training we get, any novel gets written at all.

Or that any writer even gets started writing.

And outlining seems to be the logical process when faced with all that. In fact, outlining would be the only way to let the critical brain even pretend to be smart.

When I started writing solidly, novels seemed flat impossible. I could manage a short story in an afternoon, but anything beyond that was a concrete wall of paralyzing fear.

So how did I break out of the problem of everything I had been taught?

I used to own a bookstore. One fine slow afternoon, I was sitting in the front room of my bookstore and I looked around at all the books in the room. And I had a realization that in hindsight sounds damn silly.

I realized that people, regular people, wrote all those books.

And what all those regular people did was just sit down and tell a story.

They were entertainers.

That simple.

It was no magic process that only really special English-department-anointed people could do. And if all those regular people with all those books covering the walls of my bookstore could do it, then I could do it as well.

So I looked at how I felt writing short stories.

At that point I just wrote a story and stopped when the story was over. Nothing more fancy. I figured I could do that with a novel as well.

So after that realization, over the next few years I started five or six novels and got stuck at the one-third point where I could no longer fight the critical voice into submission. I had no tools to fight the critical voice at that point in time, to be honest.

So two years after that realization, mad at myself for not finishing a novel and for making novels into something "important" instead of just fun, entertaining stories, I sat down at my trusty typewriter and thought only about writing ten pages a day.

I had no outline, nothing. My focus was on finishing ten pages. Period.

Thirty days later I had finished an 80,000-word novel.

My first written novel.

The next day, I started into a second novel, doing ten pages a day again.

I powered my way through the need, the belief, the fear of doing a novel the way it "should" be done.

And never ever had that fear again. I had other fears, sure, but not that one.

Every long-term novel writer has some story of getting past the need for major outlines, for major planning. A lot of younger professionals are still banging out outlines and following them.

Again, no right way.

But eventually, if you are going to be around for a long time and writing, you need to feed the reader part of your brain and just write for fun.

Otherwise, knowing the ending of a novel, having it all figured out ahead of time, is just too dull and boring and way too much work.

To read more, pick up a copy of *Writing into the Dark* from your favorite retailer.

ABOUT THE AUTHOR

USA Today bestselling writer Dean Wesley Smith published more than a hundred novels in thirty years and hundreds of short stories across many genres.

He wrote a couple dozen *Star Trek* novels, the only two original *Men in Black* novels, Spider-Man and X-Men novels, plus novels set in gaming and television worlds. He wrote novels under dozens of pen names in the worlds of comic books and movies, including novelizations of a dozen films, from *The Final Fantasy* to *Steel* to *Rundown*.

He now writes his own original fiction under just the one name, Dean Wesley Smith. In addition to his upcoming novel releases, his monthly magazine called *Smith's Monthly* premiered October 1, 2013, filled entirely with his original novels and stories.

Dean also worked as an editor and publisher, first at Pulphouse Publishing, then for *VB Tech Journal,* then for Pocket Books. He now plays a role as an executive editor for the original anthology series *Fiction River.*

For more information go to www.deanwesleysmith.com, www.smithsmonthly.com or www.fictionriver.com.

Lightning Source UK Ltd.
Milton Keynes UK
UKHW012035191119
353844UK00001B/9/P